People in the Community

Teachers

Diyan Leake

Heinemann Library
Chicago, Illinois

Customer Service 888-454-2279
Visit our website at www.heinemannraintree.com

Designed by Joanna Hinton-Malivoire and Steve Mead
Printed in China by South China Printing Company Limited

12 11 10 09 08
10 9 8 7 6 5 4 3 2 1

Library of Congress Cataloguing-in-Publication Data

Leake, Diyan.
  Teachers / Diyan Leake.
    p. cm. -- (People in the community)
  Includes bibliographical references and index.
  ISBN-13: 978-1-4329-1191-1 (hc)
  ISBN-13: 978-1-4329-1198-0 (pb)
  1. Teachers--Juvenile literature. I. Title.
LB1775.L365 2008
371.1--dc22

2007045072

Acknowledgments
The publishers would like to thank the following for permission to reproduce photographs:
©Age Fotostock pp. **9** (Stewart Cohen/Pam Ost), **16** (Jeff Greenberg); ©Alamy (Gapys Krzysztof) p. **12**; ©AP Photo (Tomas Munita) p. **15**; ©Corbis (Sophie Elbaz/Sygma) p. **20**; ©Getty Images pp. **4** (Fraser Hall), **5** (Amanda Hall), **6** (Paula Bronstein), **7** (Mustafa Ozer/AFP), **8** (Angelo Cavalli), **11** (Tony Metaxas), **13** (Rana Faure), **14** (T-Pool), **21** (China Photos), **22 (top)** (Rana Faure), **22 (middle)** (Fraser Hall), **22 (bottom)** (Fraser Hall), **22 (bottom)** (T-Pool); ©The Image Works (Arnold Gold/New Haven Register) p. **19**; ©Landov (Oswaldo Rivas/Reuters) p. **17**; ©Peter Arnold Inc. (Shehzad Noorani) p. **10**; ©PhotoEdit (Michael Newman) p. **18**.

Front cover photograph of a young boy counting dice at the Bohula Model Government Primary School in Habiganj Upazila in Sylhet District, Bangladesh, reproduced with permission of ©Peter Arnold Inc. (Shehzad Noorani). Back cover photograph reproduced with permission of ©Getty Images (Angelo Cavalli).

Every effort has been made to contact copyright holders of any material reproduced in this book. Any omissions will be rectified in subsequent printings if notice is given to the publisher.

Contents

Communities

People live in communities.

People work in communities.

Teachers in the Community

Teachers work in communities.

Teachers help people learn.

What Teachers Do

Teachers teach children.

Teachers teach adults.

Teachers teach reading and writing.

Teachers teach math and science.

Where Teachers Work

Teachers work in schools.

Teachers work in colleges.

What Teachers Use

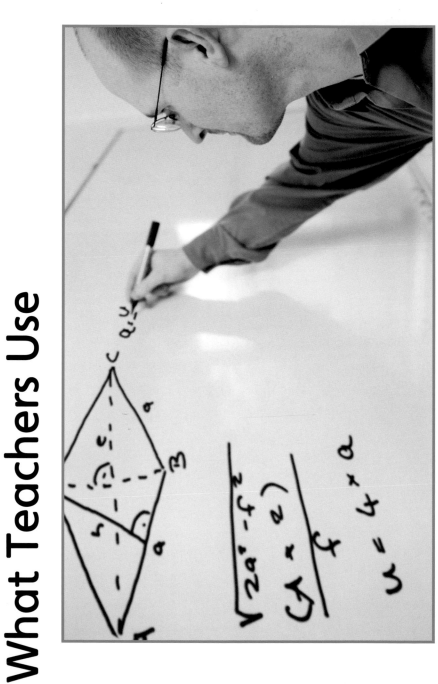

Teachers use whiteboards.

Teachers use books.

People Who Work with Teachers

Teachers work with principals.

Teachers work with other teachers.

Teachers work with parents.

Teachers work with janitors.

How Teachers Help Us

Teachers help us learn.

Teachers help the community.

Picture Glossary

college place where adults go to learn

community group of people living and working in the same area

whiteboard board that teachers write on

Index

Note to Parents and Teachers

This series introduces readers to the lives of different community workers, and explains some of the jobs they perform around the world. Some of the locations featured in this book include Cape Cod, MA (page 4); Ladakh, India (page 6); Habiganj Upazila, Bangladesh (page 10); Odessa, Ukraine (page 12); Ziarat Gali, Pakistan (page 15); Managua, Nicaragua (page 17); and Shigatse, China (page 21).

Discuss with children their experiences with teachers in the community. Ask them why they think communities need teachers. Look through the book with the class and ask children to name some of the tools teachers use to help them with their job.

The text has been chosen with the advice of a literacy expert to enable beginning readers success while reading independently or with moderate support. You can support children's nonfiction literacy skills by helping them use the table of contents, picture glossary, and index.